Light and Sound Waves

by Ana Paulinas

Sound

Bang. Beep. Buzz. Hum. Pop. Rattle. Woof. Sounds are all around you. Some, such as car horns and fire alarms, help keep you safe. Some, such as your teacher's voice and your friend's whispers, give you information. Sound is an important part of your life. But what is sound? How is it made?

Sound is a form of energy. It begins when something vibrates. This means it moves back and forth quickly. For example, if you hit a gong, the gong vibrates. You can see it moving back and forth. The vibrating gong passes energy to the air around it. Then the air vibrates too. These vibrations move through the air as sound waves. The sound waves carry energy. We hear the sound of the gong when the sound waves reach our ears.

When a gong vibrates, it creates sound waves.

Kinds of Sound Waves

Air is made up of tiny particles that you cannot see. Sound waves make these particles move. The particles bunch up and spread apart in a pattern. A **compression** is the part of the sound wave where particles are close together. Waves can be put into groups based on how they move through matter.

Sound waves make particles in the air move.

Transverse Waves

Have you ever seen ocean waves as they move toward the shore? If so, you have seen examples of transverse waves. In the ocean, the water moves up and down, yet the waves travel in a forward direction to the shore. The energy in transverse waves moves the same way. The particles in the material the wave passes through move at a right angle to the direction that the wave travels.

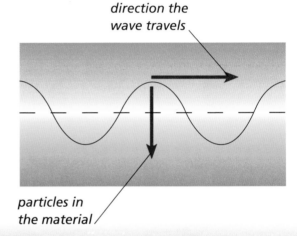

direction the wave travels

particles in the material

Ocean waves can be transverse waves. Notice how the arrows are at right angles to each other.

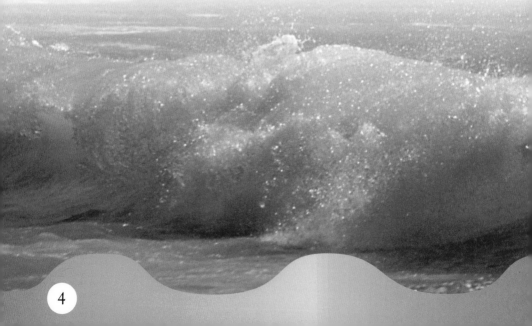

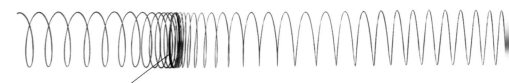

compression **Part of the spring is pressed together, and part of it is stretched out.**

Longitudinal Waves

Longitudinal waves are caused by a back-and-forth movement. Sound waves are longitudinal waves. Air particles press together and stretch out as a sound wave moves. The particles in a material move parallel to the direction of the wave. This means they move along with the wave.

Suppose you and a friend are holding the two ends of a spring. You push your end toward your friend. This sends energy and vibrations through the spring. Some of the coils crowd closer together. As the vibrations pass through the coils, they move apart.

Frequency and Wavelength

Frequency is the number of waves that pass a point in a certain amount of time. An object will have a high frequency if it vibrates quickly. A **wavelength** is the distance between two high points or two low points along the sound wave.

How many wavelengths are shown here? Count the spaces between the high points or the low points.

How does sound travel?

Sound waves travel through different states of matter at different speeds. The particles of a solid are closest together. When sound waves in a solid material vibrate, the vibration quickly moves to nearby particles. Sound waves pass quickly through a solid object.

The particles in a liquid are a little farther apart. For this reason, vibrations take a little longer to pass from one particle to another. Sound waves take a little longer to travel in a liquid.

Particles are the farthest apart in a gas. When a sound wave makes a gas particle vibrate, the particle must travel a longer distance before it bumps into another particle. When it does, that particle begins to vibrate. For this reason, sound waves travel slowest in gas.

Outer space is a vacuum. That means that it contains no matter. Since there are no particles of matter to vibrate, there is no sound in a vacuum.

gas

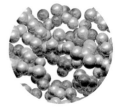

liquid

solid

Echoes

If you bounce a ball against a smooth wall, it will bounce right back toward you. Sound waves do the same thing. When sound waves hit hard, smooth surfaces, they bounce back. These bounced-back sound waves are echoes.

In the fog, boat captains can use echoes to tell how far they are from dangerous rocks and cliffs.

How Sound Is Made

Loudness

Some sounds are louder than others. For example, you know that a whisper can be difficult to hear. A scream is much louder than a whisper. But what is loudness? It's a measure of how strong a sound seems to us. It has to do with the amount of energy in a sound wave.

Suppose you are listening to the radio in your room. While you are in the room, the music seems loud. Then you go into the kitchen to get a snack. From there, you can still hear the radio, but it does not seem loud anymore. Did the loudness of the sound coming from the radio actually change? No. The radio just seems to be softer because you are farther from it. Sound waves do not lose energy as they travel through the air. The energy just spreads out over a larger area. This makes sounds seem louder or softer.

ticking watch

talking

car engine

thunder

soft   loud

Sound waves produced by thunder have more energy than sound waves produced by a ticking watch.

Pitch

Pitch is what makes a sound seem high or low. Have you ever heard the sound of chalk scratching and squeaking on a chalkboard? That is a very high sound! Have you ever heard the sound a cello makes? That's a very low sound. Objects that vibrate quickly have a high frequency. A sound with a higher frequency has a higher pitch. Objects that vibrate slowly have a low frequency and a low pitch. Keep in mind that high-pitched sounds and low-pitched sounds can be either loud or soft.

low pitch

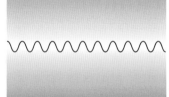

high pitch

A cello produces a low-pitched sound.

violin

drum

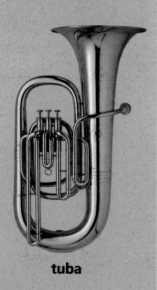

tuba

String Instruments

Musicians may pick, rub, or hit the strings on string instruments. This makes the strings vibrate. The frequency and pitch of a note depend on the length and thickness of the strings and how tightly they are stretched. Long, thick, or loose strings produce lower pitches than short, thin, or tight strings do.

Percussion Instruments

Drums, cymbals, maracas, and chimes are percussion instruments. They make sounds when they are hit or shaken. When you hit drums with drumsticks, they vibrate and make a sound.

Wind Instruments

Musicians blow air into a hole in instruments such as flutes, trumpets and tubas. The hole connects to a tube. Particles of air in the tube vibrate. The pitch that such an instrument can make depends on the length of the air tube. Air vibrates slower in a longer tube, causing a lower pitch.

Pianos

When you press a piano key, a padded hammer hits a group of strings. This makes the strings vibrate and make a sound. Pressing a piano key harder makes the sound louder. But it does not change the frequency or the pitch of the sound.

How Our Ears Work

The outer ear catches sound waves and sends them into the middle ear. The sound waves travel through the ear canal until they hit the eardrum. This makes the eardrum vibrate. Three tiny bones in the middle ear vibrate when the eardrum vibrates. The vibrations move into an area of the inner ear called the cochlea. This area is filled with liquid. Tiny hairs in the cochlea move when this liquid vibrates. The vibration of these tiny hairs sends signals to the brain. The brain understands these signals as different sounds.

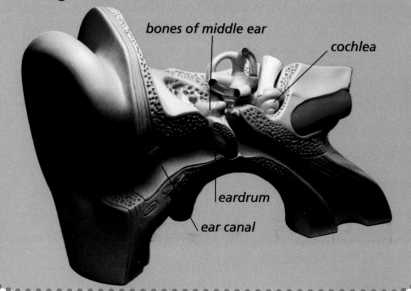

bones of middle ear

cochlea

eardrum

ear canal

Light Energy

Light is a form of energy. What is our most important source of light energy? The Sun. Without it, everything on Earth would be dead. Plants cannot grow without sunlight. Plants are an important part of the food chain. Without plants, animals and people could not survive.

Some animals give off light. This is bioluminescence. The light comes from chemical reactions inside animals.

Long ago, people found they could make fire. This meant they could have light and heat whenever they needed it—even after the Sun went down! These prehistoric people did not have any knowledge of light waves and how they work, but they knew they were very important.

The Sun gives Earth light energy.

Shadows

Light travels in straight lines called rays. Rays spread outward from a light source.

A silhouette is a kind of shadow. Look at the silhouette shown here. It shows how shadows are made. The flashlight is sending rays of light toward the puppet. Since the rays cannot go through the puppet or curve around it, a shadow appears on the wall. The shadow shows the area where light rays were blocked by the puppet.

The size of a shadow can change. If the puppet is moved closer to the flashlight, the shadow will become larger. If the puppet is farther away from the flashlight, the shadow will get smaller.

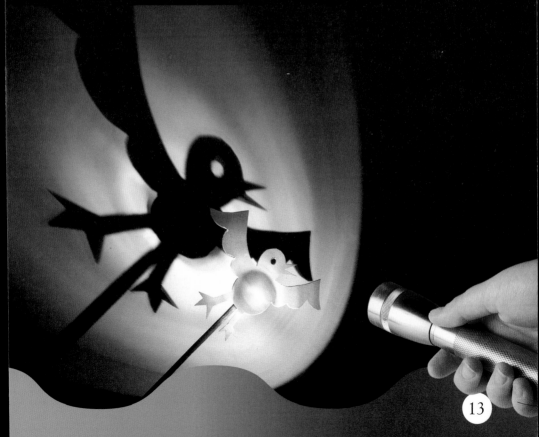

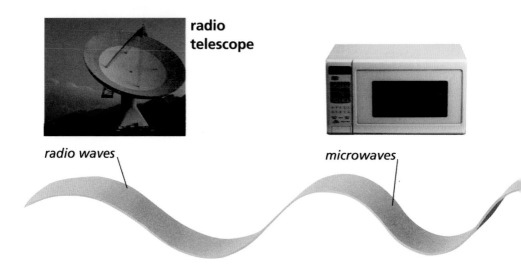

radio
telescope

radio waves

microwaves

Visible Spectrum

Similar to sound waves, light waves have wavelengths and frequencies. People can only see light that has certain wavelengths and frequencies. The visible spectrum—or the light that we can see—is only a small part of the light energy in the universe. Scientists describe all the different forms of light as the electromagnetic spectrum.

Differences in the wavelengths and frequencies make colors of light. White light, such as light from the Sun or most light bulbs, is actually a combination of the colors red, orange, yellow, green, blue, and violet. These colors make up the visible spectrum.

Look at the diagram on page 15. The colors of the visible spectrum are always in the same order because of their wavelength and frequency. As you move from left to right, wavelength decreases and frequency increases.

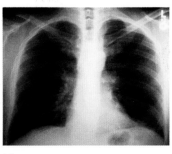

ultraviolet waves   X rays

visible spectrum

Electromagnetic Waves

Most electromagnetic waves cannot be seen by the human eye. Some wavelengths are too long to be visible. The electromagnetic waves in microwave ovens are too long for us to see. Some wavelengths are too short to be seen. That's why X rays are invisible.

Scientists can use special equipment to study invisible electromagnetic waves. These waves move in the same way as visible light waves. They all travel at the same speed through empty space. They also carry energy. Some objects can absorb this energy and change it to another form of energy, such as heat.

Living cells can be harmed by too much exposure to certain waves. Ultraviolet waves from the Sun can damage your eyes. But in smaller amounts, ultraviolet waves can kill bacteria.

Light and Matter

When light rays strike an object, the rays may pass through the object. They may reflect off the object. Or they may be absorbed by the object.

Reflection occurs when light rays bounce, or reflect, off the surface of an object and return back to our eyes. Some objects reflect light rays better than others. Mirrors and glass reflect light very well. Calm waters can also reflect light.

If you have ever walked on your driveway or on a street in bare feet on a hot summer day, you have experienced absorption. Absorption is when an object takes in light waves rather than reflecting them. Light waves become heat energy when they are absorbed.

You can see the city lights reflected in the water.

Color and Light

We see colors because objects absorb some frequencies of light and they reflect others. Do you remember reading that white light is the combination of all colors? If white light shines on objects, they absorb some of its colors and reflect others. A substance in this pepper's skin makes it absorb all the colors in white light, except red. Red light bounces off the pepper, so that is the color we see. That's why this pepper looks red.

What makes an object look white? This happens when all the colors in white light are reflected by an object and none are absorbed. The reflected colors blend again and we see white. What makes an object look black? It absorbs all the colors in white light and reflects none of them.

red pepper

Letting Light Through

One way to group materials is by how light passes through them. **Transparent** materials let nearly all light rays pass through them. Air, clean water, and glass are all transparent. You can clearly see what is on the other side of them. Transparent objects don't have to be clear with no color. They can be tinted different colors, such as the lenses in sunglasses.

Translucent materials let some light rays pass through them. Look through a piece of frosted glass or a sheet of wax paper. You can see what is on the other side, but it looks a little fuzzy.

Opaque materials don't let any light rays pass through them. You can't see through an opaque object. Some opaque materials, such as steel, reflect light rays. The light rays bounce off the steel and make it look shiny. Other opaque materials, such as brick and wood, absorb light.

Flashlights shining on each of these tubes show how different materials react to light.

transparent   translucent

How Light Moves

Light waves move slowly through objects whose particles are close together. Light moves more slowly through water than through air. It moves slowest through a solid. Light travels fastest through empty space.

When light moves at an angle from one medium to another, some of the light is absorbed, or taken in. Some of the light is reflected, or bounced back. Some of the light changes direction and bends. This bending is called **refraction.** As light rays move at an angle from one transparent medium to another, they change speed. This change in speed makes the light rays bend, or refract.

Do you notice that the pen in the water looks as though it's broken? That's what happens when light that is moving through air hits a solid transparent object (the glass) that contains a transparent liquid (the water).

opaque

Light rays refract, or bend, as they travel from air to water. That's why the pen looks as though it's broken.

The Human Eye

The human eye is a small ball filled with liquid. It has a bony area around it. A transparent covering protects the front of the eye. This covering also refracts any rays of light that enter the eye. The colored part of the eye is called the iris. The iris is a muscle behind the covering of the eye. The pupil is the dark opening in the center of the iris. The pupil and the iris work together to control how much light enters the eye.

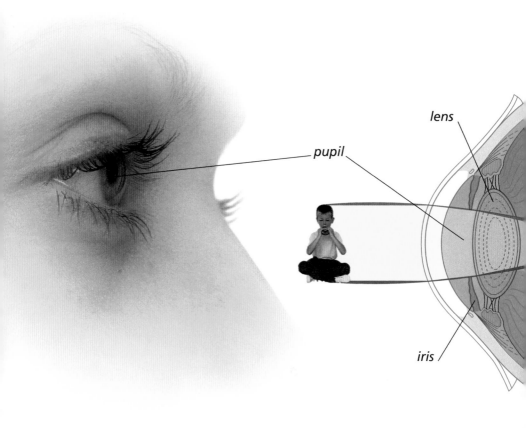

lens

pupil

iris

To protect the eye from bright light, the iris closes and the pupil gets smaller. This keeps too much light from entering the eye at once and possibly damaging it. The iris opens and the pupil gets larger when it is dark. This is to allow in as much light as possible. The light that enters the eye passes through the lens, which is behind the pupil. The lens bends the light a little more. Then the rays of light cross and form an upside-down image on the retina. The cells in the retina change the light into signals that move along the optic nerve to the brain. Then you see things right side up.

The pupil changes size to let in more or less light.

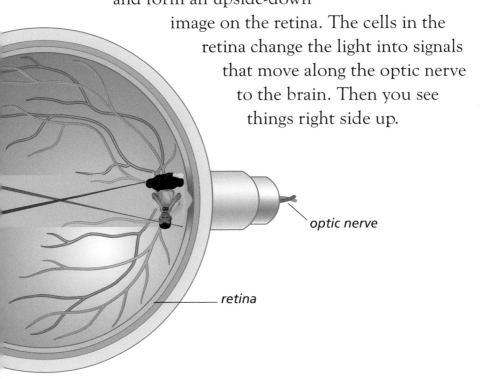

optic nerve

retina

Convex and Concave Lenses

Lenses are curved pieces of clear glass or plastic. They refract light that passes through them. There are two main kinds of lenses.

A convex lens is thicker in the middle than at the edges. Light rays bend toward the middle of the lens. These rays meet at a point on the opposite side of the lens. A convex lens can make things look bigger. Magnifying glasses and microscopes have convex lenses.

A magnifying glass has a convex lens.

Light rays bend toward the middle of a convex lens.

A concave lens is thinner in the middle than at the edges. Light rays bend out to the thicker edges of a concave lens. Then the rays spread apart. Objects seen through a concave lens look smaller than they really are.

Many kinds of telescopes use both concave and convex lenses. When they are used together, they make details sharper.

Light rays bend outward to the edges of a concave lens.

Now when you hear *bang, beep, buzz, hum, pop, rattle,* and *woof,* or when you see objects that are red, orange, yellow, green, blue, and violet, you can think of waves. You'll know not to look for them, because you can't see them. But you'll know that they are all around you.

Telescopes can use both convex and concave lenses.

Glossary

absorption   the taking in of light waves

compression   the part of a sound wave where the particles are close together

frequency   the number of waves that pass a point in a certain amount of time

opaque   allowing no light rays to pass through a material

pitch   a characteristic of sound that makes it seem high or low

reflection   the bouncing of light off a surface to our eyes

refraction   the bending of light

translucent   allowing some light rays to pass through a material

transparent   allowing nearly all light rays to pass through a material

wavelength   the distance between two high points or low points along a wave